5 INGREDIENT INSTANT MEALS

Publications International, Ltd.

Pictured on the front cover: Chicken, Broccoli and Tomato Pasta *(page 168)*.
Pictured on the back cover *(counterclockwise from top left):* Pork & Asparagus Stir-Fry *(page 124)*, Fruited Waffle Parfait Cup *(page 30)*, Saucy Mario Sandwiches *(page 68)* and Balsamic Butternut Squash *(page 102)*.

Microwave Cooking: Microwave ovens vary in wattage. Use the cooking times as guidelines and check for doneness before adding more time.

TABLE OF CONTENTS

BREAKFAST EXPRESS

BLUEBERRY PANCAKES

2 tablespoons plus
   2 teaspoons unsalted
   butter

1 egg, beaten

1¼ cups milk

1¼ cups all-purpose flour

½ cup dried blueberries

¼ cup light brown sugar or
   granulated maple sugar

1 tablespoon baking powder

Fresh blueberries (optional)

Powdered sugar or maple
syrup

1. Melt butter in large heavy-bottomed skillet or griddle over medium heat. Pour into medium bowl, leaving thin film of butter on skillet. Mix egg and milk into butter in bowl.

2. Combine flour, dried blueberries, brown sugar and baking powder in large bowl; stir to blend. Add egg mixture; stir to blend. ***Do not beat.*** Pour ¼-cup portions of batter into skillet. Cook over medium heat 2 to 3 minutes on each side or until golden. Serve with fresh blueberries, if desired. Dust with powdered sugar.

MAKES 10 TO 12 PANCAKES

SMOKED SALMON HASH BROWNS

3 cups frozen hash brown potatoes, thawed

2 pouches (3 ounces each) smoked salmon*

½ cup chopped onion

½ cup chopped green bell pepper

¼ teaspoon black pepper

2 tablespoons vegetable oil

Fresh fruit (optional)

Sprigs fresh mint (optional)

Smoked salmon in foil pouches can be found in the canned fish section of the supermarket. Do not substitute lox or other fresh smoked salmon.

1. Combine potatoes, salmon, onion, bell pepper and black pepper in large bowl; mix well.

2. Heat oil in large skillet over medium-high heat. Add potato mixture; pat down evenly.

3. Cook 5 minutes or until bottom is crisp and brown. Turn over in large pieces. Cook 2 to 3 minutes or until both sides are browned. Serve with fruit, if desired. Garnish with mint.

MAKES 4 SERVINGS

HARVEST APPLE OATMUG

1 cup water

½ cup old-fashioned oats

½ cup chopped Granny Smith apple

2 tablespoons raisins

1 teaspoon packed brown sugar

¼ teaspoon ground cinnamon

⅛ teaspoon salt

MICROWAVE DIRECTIONS

1. Combine water, oats, apple, raisins, brown sugar, cinnamon and salt in large microwavable mug; mix well.

2. Microwave on HIGH 1½ minutes; stir. Microwave on HIGH 1 minute or until thickened and liquid is absorbed. Let stand 1 to 2 minutes before serving.

MAKES 1 SERVING

MEDITERRANEAN ARTICHOKE OMELET

2 eggs

1 tablespoon grated Parmesan cheese

2 tablespoons olive oil

3 cans (14 ounces each) artichoke bottoms packed in water, drained and diced

1 ounce (about 2 pieces) roasted red bell peppers, diced

½ teaspoon minced garlic

1 tablespoon tomato salsa

1. Beat eggs well in small bowl. Stir in cheese.

2. Heat oil in large skillet over medium-high heat. Add artichokes; cook and stir 2 to 3 minutes or until beginning to brown. Add bell peppers; cook and stir 2 minutes or until liquid has evaporated. Add garlic; cook and stir 30 seconds. Remove to small plate; keep warm.

3. Add egg mixture to skillet. Lift edge of omelet with spatula to allow uncooked portion to flow underneath. Cook 1 to 2 minutes or until omelet is almost set.

4. Spoon artichoke mixture onto half of omelet; fold omelet over filling. Cook 2 minutes or until set. Serve with salsa.

MAKES 1 SERVING

NOTE: Raw eggs will turn green if combined with raw artichokes because of a chemical reaction between the two foods. Cooking the artichokes separately will prevent this from happening.

BERRY MORNING MEDLEY

1   cup frozen mixed berries

1½   cups milk

½   cup plain nonfat yogurt

1   tablespoon sugar

¼   teaspoon vanilla

¼   cup granola, plus additional
     for garnish

1. Combine berries and milk in blender; blend until mixture is thick and creamy.

2. Add yogurt, sugar and vanilla; blend until smooth. Add ¼ cup granola; pulse 15 to 20 seconds.

3. Pour into two glasses. Sprinkle additional granola on top, if desired.

MAKES 2 SERVINGS

AREPAS (LATIN AMERICAN CORN CAKES)

1½ cups instant corn flour for arepas*

½ teaspoon salt

1½ to 2 cups hot water

⅓ cup shredded Mexican cheese blend

1 tablespoon butter, melted

May also be called masarepa, masa al instante and harina precodica. It is not the same as masa harina or regular cornmeal. Purchase arepa flour at Latin American markets or online.

1. Preheat oven to 350°F. Combine instant corn flour and salt in medium bowl. Stir in 1½ cups hot water. Dough should be smooth and moist but not sticky; add more water, 1 tablespoon at a time, if necessary. Add cheese and butter. Knead until dough is consistency of smooth mashed potatoes.

2. Lightly grease heavy skillet or griddle; heat over medium heat. Divide dough into 6 to 8 equal pieces; flatten and pat dough into 4-inch discs ½ inch thick. (If dough cracks or is too dry, return to bowl and add additional water, 1 tablespoon at a time.)

3. Immediately place dough pieces in hot skillet. Cook 3 to 5 minutes per side or until browned in spots. Remove to baking sheet.

4. Bake 15 minutes or until arepas sound hollow when tapped. Serve warm.

5. If desired, make breakfast sandwiches by splitting arepas with a fork as you would English muffins. Fill with eggs, cheese and salsa as desired.

MAKES 6 TO 8 AREPAS

STRAWBERRY-TOPPED WAFFLES WITH SWEET AND CREAMY SAUCE

3 ounces cream cheese

¼ cup half-and-half

2 tablespoons sugar

¼ teaspoon vanilla

4 frozen waffles

1 cup sliced fresh
   strawberries

1. Combine cream cheese, half-and-half, sugar and vanilla in food processor or blender; blend until smooth.

2. Toast waffles. Spoon sauce over waffles; top with strawberries.

MAKES 4 SERVINGS

FRENCH TOAST

2 eggs, lightly beaten

½ cup milk

½ teaspoon WATKINS® Vanilla

¼ teaspoon salt

6 slices day-old bread

1 tablespoon butter

Combine eggs, milk, vanilla and salt in shallow bowl; mix well. Dip bread slices in egg mixture. Melt butter in large skillet; cook bread until golden brown on both sides. Serve hot with maple syrup, powdered sugar or tart jelly.

MAKES 3 SERVINGS

STRAWBERRY-TOPPED WAFFLES
WITH SWEET AND CREAMY SAUCE

HAM & SWISS CHEESE BISCUITS

2 cups all-purpose flour

2 teaspoons baking powder

½ teaspoon baking soda

½ cup (1 stick) butter, cut into small pieces

⅔ cup buttermilk

½ cup (2 ounces) shredded Swiss cheese

2 ounces ham, minced

1. Preheat oven to 450°F. Spray large baking sheet with nonstick cooking spray.

2. Combine flour, baking powder and baking soda in medium bowl. Cut in butter with pastry blender or two knives until mixture resembles coarse crumbs. Stir in buttermilk, 1 tablespoon at a time, until slightly sticky dough forms. Stir in cheese and ham.

3. Turn out dough onto lightly floured surface; knead lightly. Roll out dough to ½ inch thick. Cut out biscuits with 2-inch round cutter. Place on prepared baking sheet.

4. Bake 10 minutes or until browned. Serve warm.

MAKES ABOUT 18 BISCUITS

BREAKFAST QUESADILLAS

1 pound BOB EVANS® Original Recipe Roll Sausage

4 eggs

4 (10-inch) flour tortillas

2 cups (8 ounces) shredded Monterey Jack cheese

½ cup chopped green onions with tops

½ cup chopped tomato

Sour cream and salsa

Crumble sausage into large skillet. Cook over medium heat until sausage is browned, stirring occasionally. Drain off any drippings. Remove sausage to paper towels; set aside. Add eggs to same skillet; scramble until eggs are set but not dry. Remove eggs; set aside. Place 1 tortilla in same skillet. Top with half of *each* eggs, cheese, sausage, onions and tomato. Heat until cheese melts; top with another tortilla. Remove from skillet; cut into six equal wedges. Repeat with remaining tortillas, eggs, cheese, sausage, onions and tomato to make second quesadilla. Serve warm with sour cream and salsa. Refrigerate any leftovers.

MAKES 4 SERVINGS

BANANA SPLIT BREAKFAST BOWL

2½ tablespoons sliced almonds

2½ tablespoons chopped walnuts

3 cups vanilla nonfat yogurt

1⅓ cups sliced fresh strawberries (about 12 medium)

2 bananas, sliced

½ cup drained pineapple tidbits

1. Combine almonds and walnuts in small skillet; cook and stir over medium heat 2 minutes or until lightly browned. Immediately remove from skillet; cool completely.

2. Spoon yogurt into serving bowls. Layer with strawberries, bananas and pineapple; sprinkle with toasted almonds and walnuts.

MAKES 4 SERVINGS

NOTE: This breakfast bowl can also be made with frozen strawberries. Frozen fruits are economical, convenient and available year-round. They have been harvested at the peak of ripeness and can be stored in the freezer for 8 to 12 months.

SCRAMBLED EGGS WITH SMOKED SALMON

8 eggs

⅛ teaspoon black pepper

2 tablespoons sliced green onions, with tops

1 ounce chilled cream cheese, cut into ¼-inch cubes

2 ounces smoked salmon, flaked

1. Whisk eggs and pepper in large bowl. Spray large skillet with nonstick cooking spray; heat over medium heat. Pour eggs into skillet; cook and stir 5 to 7 minutes or until mixture begins to set.

2. Gently fold in green onions, cream cheese and salmon; cook and stir 3 minutes or just until eggs are cooked through but still slightly moist.

MAKES 4 SERVINGS

DEEP SOUTH HAM AND REDEYE GRAVY

1 tablespoon butter

1 ham steak (about 1⅓ pounds)

1 cup strong coffee

¾ teaspoon sugar

¼ teaspoon hot pepper sauce

1. Heat large skillet over medium-high heat. Add butter; tilt skillet to coat bottom. Add ham steak; cook 3 minutes. Turn; cook 2 minutes or until lightly browned. Remove ham to serving platter; keep warm.

2. Add coffee, sugar and hot pepper sauce to same skillet. Bring to a boil over high heat; boil 3 minutes or until liquid is reduced to ¼ cup, scraping up any brown bits from bottom of skillet. Serve gravy over ham steak.

MAKES 4 TO 6 SERVINGS

DEVIL'S FOOD PANCAKES

Strawberry Topping
(recipe follows, optional)

1 package (about 15 ounces)
devil's food cake mix

2 cups milk

2 eggs

½ cup mini semisweet
chocolate chips

Powdered sugar

1. Prepare Strawberry Topping, if desired.

2. Whisk cake mix, milk and eggs in large bowl until well blended. Stir in chocolate chips.

3. Heat griddle or large nonstick skillet over medium-low to medium heat.* Pour ¼ cupfuls batter onto skillet. Cook 3 to 4 minutes or until edges appear dry; turn and cook 3 minutes.

4. Sprinkle with powdered sugar and serve with Strawberry Topping, if desired.

If using electric griddle, do not cook pancakes at higher than 350°F as they burn easily.

MAKES ABOUT 22 (4-INCH) PANCAKES

STRAWBERRY TOPPING: Combine 1 cup chopped fresh strawberries and ⅓ cup strawberry preserves in medium bowl; mix well.

NOTE: These pancakes freeze well. Freeze four pancakes in one resealable food storage bag. Reheat in the microwave oven as needed.

SAWMILL BISCUITS AND GRAVY

- 3 tablespoons canola or vegetable oil, divided
- 8 ounces bulk breakfast sausage
- 2¼ cups plus 3 tablespoons biscuit baking mix, divided
- 2⅔ cups whole milk, divided
- ¼ teaspoon salt
- ¼ teaspoon black pepper
- Fresh fruit (optional)

1. Preheat oven to 450°F. Heat 1 tablespoon oil in large skillet over medium heat. Add sausage; cook and stir 6 to 8 minutes or until browned, stirring to break up meat. Remove to plate using slotted spoon.

2. Add remaining 2 tablespoons oil to skillet. Add 3 tablespoons biscuit mix; whisk until smooth. Gradually add 2 cups milk; cook and stir 3 to 4 minutes or until mixture comes to a boil. Cook and stir 1 minute or until thickened. Add sausage and any juices; cook and stir 2 minutes. Season with salt and pepper.

3. Combine remaining 2¼ cups biscuit mix and ⅔ cup milk in medium bowl; stir until blended. Spoon batter into eight mounds onto gravy mixture.

4. Bake 8 to 10 minutes or until golden. Serve warm with gravy. Serve with fruit, if desired.

MAKES 8 SERVINGS

FRUITED WAFFLE PARFAIT CUP

1 cooked or leftover Belgian waffle, torn into bite-sized pieces

½ cup raspberry jam

½ teaspoon almond extract

1 cup plain or vanilla yogurt

2 cups chopped fresh peaches or frozen peaches, thawed

1. Place equal amounts of waffle pieces in each of four parfait dishes.

2. Place jam in small microwave-safe bowl; microwave on HIGH 30 seconds to slightly melt. Stir in almond extract until smooth. Spoon over waffle pieces; top with yogurt and fruit.

MAKES 4 SERVINGS

APPLE CINNAMON SANDWICHES

¼ cup cream cheese

8 slices whole grain cinnamon raisin bread

1 medium Granny Smith apple (about 5 ounces), thinly sliced

¼ cup red raspberry preserves

⅛ teaspoon ground cinnamon

2 tablespoons butter

1. Spread 1 tablespoon cream cheese on opposite side of four bread slices. Arrange apple slices over cream cheese. Spread 1 tablespoon preserves on remaining four bread slices; sprinkle with cinnamon. Place bread slices together to make sandwiches.

2. Melt butter in large skillet over medium heat. Add sandwiches; cook 2 to 3 minutes on each side or until golden brown.

MAKES 4 SERVINGS

DUAL-COLORED MEXICAN EGGS

2 to 4 tablespoons butter

16 eggs

8 ORTEGA® Tostada Shells

1 cup ORTEGA® Salsa, any variety

1 cup ORTEGA® Salsa Verde

1 cup crumbled queso fresco or feta cheese

MELT ½ to 1 tablespoon butter in medium nonstick skillet over medium heat; swirl melted butter to coat bottom of skillet.

BREAK 2 eggs into cup or small bowl. Slide eggs into skillet. Cook, uncovered, 3 to 4 minutes, until egg whites are set and yolks reach desired doneness.

PLACE tostada shell on serving plate; top with fried eggs. Drizzle ¼ cup desired salsa over eggs. Crumble cheese evenly over eggs.

REPEAT with remaining butter, eggs, tostadas, salsas and cheese. Serve immediately.

MAKES 8 SERVINGS

TIP: To enjoy a different taste sensation, try both salsas at once. Spoon 2 tablespoons salsa over one egg and 2 tablespoons salsa verde over the other egg before sprinkling with cheese.

BERRY-BANANA BREAKFAST SMOOTHIE

1 container (6 ounces)
   berry-flavored yogurt

1 ripe banana, sliced

½ cup milk

Combine yogurt, banana and milk in blender; blend until smooth. Pour into two glasses. Serve immediately.

MAKES 2 SERVINGS

BANANA-PINEAPPLE BREAKFAST SHAKE

2 cups plain nonfat yogurt

1 can (8 ounces) crushed
   pineapple in juice,
   undrained

1 ripe medium banana

¼ cup sugar

1 teaspoon vanilla

⅛ teaspoon ground nutmeg

1 cup ice cubes

1. Combine yogurt, pineapple, banana, sugar, vanilla, nutmeg and ice in blender; blend until smooth.

2. Pour into four glasses. Serve immediately.

MAKES 4 SERVINGS

TIP: This recipe is perfect for a brunch, a party or another special occasion. Make as many batches as you need to serve everyone.

BERRY-BANANA
BREAKFAST SMOOTHIE

MICROWAVED OATS CEREAL

1¾ cups water

⅓ cup old-fashioned oats

⅓ cup oat bran

1 tablespoon packed brown sugar

¼ teaspoon ground cinnamon

⅛ teaspoon salt

MICROWAVE DIRECTIONS

1. Combine water, oats, oat bran, brown sugar, cinnamon and salt in large microwavable bowl (cereal expands rapidly when it cooks). Cover with vented plastic wrap.

2. Microwave on HIGH about 6 minutes or until thickened. Stir well. Let stand 2 minutes before serving.

MAKES 2 SERVINGS

SERVING SUGGESTION: To boost the flavor for this quick morning meal, add fresh blueberries or strawberries, or top with chopped nuts and dried cherries.

BUCKWHEAT BROWNS

1 cup cooked soba noodles, drained and chopped well

⅓ cup bacon, crisp-cooked and crumbled

⅓ cup minced fresh parsley

¼ cup minced red bell pepper

1 teaspoon minced garlic

1 egg white, beaten until foamy

½ teaspoon black pepper

1. Combine noodles, bacon, parsley, bell pepper, garlic and egg white in medium bowl; stir well. Add black pepper; stir. (Egg white will be partially absorbed.)

2. Spray large skillet with nonstick cooking spray; heat over medium-high heat. Use ¼ cup measure to scoop noodle mixture onto skillet. Cook 3 to 4 minutes. Spray each noodle cluster with cooking spray; turn and cook 3 to 4 minutes or until noodles are browned at edges. Serve warm.

MAKES 6 SERVINGS

HAWAIIAN BREAKFAST PIZZA

2 teaspoons pineapple jam

1 English muffin, split and toasted

1 slice (1 ounce) smoked ham, diced

½ cup pineapple tidbits, drained

2 tablespoons shredded Cheddar cheese

1. Preheat toaster oven. Spread jam over each muffin half; place on foil-lined toaster oven tray. Sprinkle ham and pineapple tidbits over muffin halves; top with cheese.

2. Toast 2 minutes or until cheese is melted.

MAKES 1 SERVING

NOTE: To heat in a conventional oven, preheat oven to 400°F. Heat muffin halves on a foil-lined baking sheet 5 minutes or until cheese is melted.

CRISPY SKILLET POTATOES

2 tablespoons olive oil

4 red potatoes, cut into thin wedges

½ cup chopped onion

2 tablespoons lemon-pepper seasoning

½ teaspoon coarse salt

Chopped fresh parsley (optional)

Scrambled eggs (optional)

1. Heat oil in large cast iron skillet over medium heat. Stir in potatoes, onion, lemon-pepper seasoning and salt. Cover and cook 25 to 30 minutes or until potatoes are tender and browned, turning occasionally.

2. Sprinkle with parsley just before serving. Serve with scrambled eggs, if desired.

MAKES 4 SERVINGS

QUICK BREAKFAST SANDWICH

2 turkey breakfast sausage patties

3 eggs

Salt and black pepper

2 teaspoons butter

2 slices Cheddar cheese

2 whole wheat English muffins, split and toasted

1. Cook sausage according to package directions; keep warm.

2. Beat eggs, salt and pepper in small bowl. Melt butter in small skillet over low heat. Pour eggs into skillet; cook and stir just until set.

3. Place cheese on bottom halves of English muffins; top with sausage and scrambled eggs. Serve immediately.

MAKES 2 SANDWICHES

SANDWICHES & SALADS

THE GREAT REUBEN SANDWICH

¼ cup Thousand Island dressing (see Tip)

4 slices rye bread

8 ounces thinly sliced corned beef or pastrami

4 slices Swiss cheese

½ cup sauerkraut, well drained

2 tablespoons butter

1. Spread dressing on one side of each bread slice. Top 2 bread slices with corned beef, cheese, sauerkraut and remaining bread slices.

2. Melt butter in large skillet over medium heat. Add sandwiches; press down with spatula or weigh down with small plate. Cook sandwiches 6 minutes per side or until cheese is melted and bread is lightly browned, pressing down with spatula to crisp bread slightly. Serve immediately.

MAKES 2 SANDWICHES

TIP: If you don't have Thousand Island dressing, you can make your own by combining 2 tablespoons mayonnaise, 2 tablespoons sweet pickle relish and 1 tablespoon cocktail sauce.

MINI SHRIMP SALAD ROLLS

¼ cup mayonnaise

1 teaspoon chopped fresh dill

1 teaspoon fresh lemon juice

1 teaspoon hot pepper sauce

3 cups chopped cooked shrimp
(about 1 pound)

1 package (12 ounces) sweet
Hawaiian dinner rolls, split

6 lettuce leaves, torn in half

1. Stir mayonnaise, dill, lemon juice and hot pepper sauce in medium bowl until well blended. Add shrimp; gently mix to coat evenly.

2. To assemble, layer bottoms of rolls with lettuce, shrimp salad and tops of rolls.

MAKES 12 SERVINGS

PICO DE GALLO SHRIMP & AVOCADO SALAD

2 tablespoons canola oil

1 pound extra large shrimp,
peeled and deveined

1 jar (16 ounces) PACE® Pico de
Gallo

8 cups mixed salad greens

1 medium ripe avocado, peeled,
pitted and sliced (about
½ cup)

Prepared ranch salad dressing

1. Heat the oil in a 12-inch nonstick skillet over medium-high heat. Add the shrimp and cook until they're cooked through, stirring often. Pour off any oil. Add **1 cup** pico de gallo and toss to coat.

2. Divide the salad greens among **4** bowls. Spoon the shrimp mixture over the greens and top with the avocado. Serve with the dressing and remaining pico de gallo.

MAKES 4 SERVINGS

SPINACH & ROASTED PEPPER PANINI

1 loaf (12 ounces) focaccia

1½ cups spinach leaves (about 12 leaves)

1 jar (about 7 ounces) roasted red peppers, drained

4 slices fontina cheese

¾ cup thinly sliced red onion

Olive oil

1. Cut focaccia in half horizontally. Layer bottom half with spinach, peppers, cheese and onion. Cover with top half of focaccia. Brush outsides of sandwich lightly with oil. Cut sandwich into four equal pieces.

2. Heat large nonstick skillet over medium heat. Add sandwiches; press down lightly with spatula or weigh down with plate. Cook sandwiches 4 to 5 minutes per side or until cheese is melted and sandwiches are golden brown.

MAKES 4 SERVINGS

NOTE: Focaccia can be found in the bakery section of most supermarkets. It is often available in different flavors, such as tomato, herb, cheese or onion.

TEX-MEX FLANK STEAK SALAD

½ pound beef flank steak

½ teaspoon Mexican seasoning blend or chili powder

⅛ teaspoon salt

4 cups mixed salad greens

1 can (11 ounces) mandarin orange sections, drained

2 tablespoons green taco sauce

1. Cut flank steak lengthwise in half, then crosswise into thin strips. Combine Mexican seasoning and salt in medium bowl. Add steak strips; toss to coat.

2. Spray large skillet with olive oil cooking spray. Heat over medium-high heat. Add steak; cook and stir 1 to 2 minutes or until desired doneness.

3. Toss salad greens with orange sections in large bowl. Arrange on serving plates. Top with warm steak; drizzle with taco sauce.

MAKES 2 SERVINGS

BAVARIAN PRETZEL SANDWICHES

4 frozen soft pretzels, thawed

1 tablespoon German mustard

2 teaspoons mayonnaise

8 slices Black Forest ham

4 slices Gouda cheese

1 tablespoon water

Coarse pretzel salt

1. Preheat oven to 350°F. Line large baking sheet with parchment paper.

2. Carefully slice each pretzel in half crosswise using serrated knife. Combine mustard and mayonnaise in small bowl. Spread mustard mixture onto bottom halves of pretzels. Top with 2 slices ham, 1 slice cheese and top halves of pretzels.

3. Place sandwiches on prepared baking sheet. Brush tops of sandwiches with water; sprinkle with salt. Bake 8 minutes or until cheese is melted.

MAKES 4 SANDWICHES

THAI-STYLE WARM NOODLE SALAD

8 ounces uncooked angel hair pasta

½ cup chunky peanut butter

¼ cup soy sauce

¼ to ½ teaspoon red pepper flakes

2 green onions, thinly sliced

1 carrot, shredded

1. Cook pasta according to package directions.

2. Meanwhile, blend peanut butter, soy sauce and red pepper flakes in large serving bowl until smooth.

3. Drain pasta, reserving 5 tablespoons water. Mix hot pasta water with peanut butter mixture until smooth; toss pasta with sauce. Stir in green onions and carrot. Serve warm or at room temperature.

MAKES 4 SERVINGS

NOTES: This salad is as versatile as it is easy to make. It can be prepared a day ahead and served warm or cold—perfect for potlucks, picnics and even lunch boxes. You can also make it into a heartier meal by mixing in any leftover chicken or beef.

BACON BURGERS

8 slices bacon, crisp-cooked and divided

4 pounds ground beef

1½ teaspoons chopped fresh thyme *or* ½ teaspoon dried thyme

½ teaspoon salt

Dash black pepper

4 slices Swiss cheese

4 Asiago rolls, split

1. Prepare grill for direct cooking. Crumble 4 slices bacon.

2. Combine beef, crumbled bacon, thyme, salt and pepper in medium bowl; mix lightly. Shape into four patties.

3. Grill patties over medium-high heat, covered, 8 to 10 minutes (or uncovered, 13 to 15 minutes) until cooked through (160°F) or to desired doneness, turning occasionally. Top with cheese during last 2 minutes of grilling. Serve with remaining bacon slices on rolls.

MAKES 4 SERVINGS

SIZZLIN' BURGERS

1 pound ground beef

¼ cup FRENCH'S® Worcestershire Sauce

½ teaspoon garlic salt

1. Combine ground beef, Worcestershire and garlic salt; shape into 4 burgers.

2. Grill over medium heat for 15 minutes or until no longer pink in center, turning once.

3. Serve burgers on rolls. Splash on more Worcestershire to taste.

MAKES 4 SERVINGS

MEDITERRANEAN PASTA SALAD

12 ounces uncooked rotini pasta

1 bottle (8 ounces) Italian vinaigrette, divided

1 can (about 6 ounces) tuna packed in water, drained

3 hard-cooked eggs, peeled and cut into wedges

1 cup frozen green beans, thawed

¼ cup pitted black olives

1. Cook pasta according to package directions; drain.

2. Reserve ¼ cup vinaigrette. Toss pasta with remaining vinaigrette; place on serving platter or on individual plates.

3. Arrange tuna, eggs, green beans and olives on top of pasta. Drizzle with reserved vinaigrette. Serve chilled or at room temperature.

MAKES 6 SERVINGS

SERVE IT WITH STYLE!: Serve with an easy, flavor-boosting garnish: parsley-dipped lemon wedges. Place parsley in small bowl and dip cut edge of each lemon wedge into parsley to coat lemon.

SOUTHWEST TURKEY SANDWICH

½ cup mayonnaise

1 tablespoon minced chipotle pepper in adobo sauce

1½ teaspoons lime juice

1 round loaf (16 ounces) cheese focaccia or cheese bread (preferably Asiago cheese)

1½ cups mixed greens

12 ounces sliced smoked turkey

½ red onion, thinly sliced

1. Combine mayonnaise, chipotle pepper and lime juice in small bowl; mix well.

2. Cut loaf in half horizontally; spread cut sides of bread with mayonnaise mixture. Top bottom half of loaf with mixed greens, turkey, onion and top half of bread. Cut into wedges.

MAKES 4 SERVINGS

TROPICAL TURKEY MELT

1 English muffin, split

1 teaspoon Dijon mustard

3 slices (about 3 ounces) smoked turkey

3 thin slices papaya

1 slice Monterey Jack cheese

1. Spread inside of muffin halves with mustard. On bottom half, layer turkey, papaya and cheese. Press remaining muffin half, mustard-side down, over cheese.

2. Spray small skillet with butter-flavored cooking spray. Cook sandwich over medium heat 4 minutes or until lightly toasted. Turn; cook 4 minutes or until lightly toasted and cheese is melted.

MAKES 1 SERVING

SOUTHWEST TURKEY
SANDWICH

SALMON CAESAR SALAD

1   skinless salmon fillet
    (4 ounces)

3   cups chopped romaine
    lettuce

    Prepared croutons

1   teaspoon grated Parmesan
    cheese

1   tablespoon creamy Caesar
    salad dressing

1. Spray small skillet with nonstick cooking spray; heat over medium heat. Add salmon; cook 4 minutes per side or until salmon flakes easily when tested with fork. When cool enough to handle, cut into bite-size pieces.

2. Arrange lettuce on plate. Top with salmon, croutons and cheese.

3. Just before serving, drizzle with dressing.

MAKES 1 SERVING

TUSCAN BREAD SALAD

¼   cup prepared fat free red wine
    vinaigrette dressing

1   cup PEPPERIDGE FARM® Whole
    Grain Seasoned Croutons

2   medium tomatoes, diced
    (about 2 cups)

½   cup cubed fresh mozzarella
    cheese

2   green onions, thinly sliced
    (about ¼ cup)

6   fresh basil leaves, cut into thin
    strips **or** torn into small pieces

Pour the dressing into a medium bowl. Add the croutons, tomatoes, cheese, onions and basil and toss to coat.

MAKES 2 SERVINGS

PIZZA SANDWICH

1 loaf (12 ounces) focaccia

½ cup pizza sauce

20 slices pepperoni

8 slices mozzarella cheese

1 can (2¼ ounces) sliced
mushrooms, drained

Red pepper flakes
(optional)

Olive oil

1. Cut focaccia horizontally in half. Spread cut sides of both halves with pizza sauce. Layer bottom half with pepperoni, cheese and mushrooms; sprinkle with red pepper flakes, if desired. Cover with top half of focaccia. Brush sandwich lightly with oil.

2. Heat large nonstick skillet over medium heat. Add sandwich; press down with spatula or weigh down with small plate. Cook sandwich 4 to 5 minutes per side or until cheese is melted and sandwich is golden brown. Cut into wedges to serve.

MAKES 4 TO 6 SERVINGS

QUICK & EASY CHICKEN PESTO SALAD

1   package (3 ounces) ramen
    noodles, any flavor,
    broken into 4 large
    chunks*

1   cup chopped cooked
    chicken

½   cup halved grape
    tomatoes

¼   cup slivered or finely
    chopped carrots

1   to 2 tablespoons prepared
    pesto

    Salt and black pepper

    Discard seasoning packet.

1. Prepare noodles according to package directions. Rinse and drain under cool running water.

2. Combine noodles, chicken, tomatoes, carrots and pesto in large bowl; toss to coat. Season with salt and pepper.

MAKES 2 SERVINGS

SAUCY MARIO SANDWICHES

1 pound ground beef

2 cups PREGO® Traditional Italian Sauce, any variety

¼ cup grated Parmesan cheese

6 PEPPERIDGE FARM® Classic Hamburger Buns, split

1. Cook the beef in a 10-inch skillet over medium-high heat until the beef is well browned, stirring frequently to separate meat. Pour off any fat.

2. Stir the sauce and cheese into the skillet. Cook until the mixture is hot and bubbling.

3. Divide the beef mixture among the buns.

MAKES 6 SERVINGS

JARLSBERG® CUBANO SANDWICH

1 loaf Cuban style bread*

Yellow mustard

½ pound each baked ham and roast pork, thinly sliced

8 thin dill pickle slices

½ pound JARLSBERG® or JARLSBERG® Lite cheese, thinly sliced

*Italian or French bread can be substituted.

Slice loaf horizontally to open; spread thin layer of mustard on top and bottom halves. Arrange ham, pork, pickles and JARLSBERG® on bottom half; cover with top half and slice to make 4 sandwiches. Grill each in hot buttered pan and, using heavy iron skillet or bacon press, flatten sandwich to about ¼ of its original size. Grill each side about 2 to 3 minutes.

MAKES 4 SANDWICHES

CRUNCHY RAMEN CHICKEN SALAD

2 cups chopped cooked chicken (about 4 ounces)

1 package (8 ounces) broccoli slaw mix or coleslaw mix

1 can (11 ounces) mandarin oranges in light syrup, drained

¼ cup coleslaw dressing

1 package (3 ounces) ramen noodles, any flavor, crumbled*

Discard seasoning packet.

1. Combine chicken, slaw mix, oranges and dressing in medium bowl; toss to blend. Cover and refrigerate until ready to serve.

2. Just before serving, stir in crumbled noodles.

MAKES 4 SERVINGS

AWESOME GRILLED CHEESE SANDWICHES

1 package (11.25 ounces) PEPPERIDGE FARM® Garlic Texas Toast

6 slices fontina cheese **or** mozzarella cheese

6 thin slices deli smoked turkey

3 thin slices prosciutto

1 jar (12 ounces) sliced roasted red pepper, drained

1. Heat a panini or sandwich press according to the manufacturer's directions until hot. (Or, use a cast-iron skillet or ridged grill pan.)

2. Top **3** of the bread slices with **half** of the cheese, turkey, prosciutto, peppers and remaining cheese. Top with the remaining bread slices.

3. Put the sandwiches on the press, closing the lid onto the sandwiches. Cook the sandwiches for 5 minutes (if cooking in a skillet or grill pan, press with a spatula occasionally or weigh down with another cast-iron skillet/foil-covered brick), until lightly browned and the bread is crisp and the cheese melts.

MAKES 3 SERVINGS

KITCHEN TIP: For a spicier flavor, add a dash of crushed red pepper flakes on the cheese when assembling the sandwiches.

MILD CURRY CHICKEN SALAD WITH FRUIT

2 cups (1 pint) prepared creamy chicken salad

2 teaspoons sugar

1½ to 2 teaspoons curry powder

⅛ teaspoon ground red pepper (optional)

8 slices fresh pineapple, cut into wedges

Combine chicken salad, sugar, curry powder and ground red pepper, if desired, in medium bowl; stir gently until well blended. Spoon salad and pineapple evenly onto plates.

MAKES 4 SERVINGS

NOTE: The curry in this dish is mild, so adjust it to taste before serving.

VARIATION: Add 2 tablespoons *each* currants, chopped apples, sliced red grapes, sliced green onions, and/or toasted, slivered almonds. Serve on a bed of spring greens or baby spinach leaves.

COOK'S TIP: Some find the taste of curry harsh and prefer it cooked or toasted. To toast, heat a small nonstick skillet over medium-high heat. Add the curry powder and stir or tilt pan constantly to prevent burning. Cook just until fragrant, about 1 minute. Immediately remove from skillet.

GRILLED SALSA TURKEY BURGER

3 ounces ground turkey

1 tablespoon crushed baked tortilla chips

1 tablespoon mild or medium salsa, plus additional for topping

1 slice Monterey Jack cheese (optional)

1 whole wheat hamburger bun, split

Green leaf lettuce

1. Prepare grill for direct cooking. Lightly spray grid with nonstick cooking spray.

2. Combine turkey, chips and 1 tablespoon salsa in small bowl; mix lightly. Shape into a patty.

3. Grill burger over medium-high heat about 6 minutes per side or until cooked through (165°F). Top with cheese, if desired, during last 2 minutes of grilling. Toast bun on grill, cut sides down, during last 2 minutes of grilling.

4. Place lettuce on bottom half of bun; top with burger, additional salsa, if desired, and top half of bun.

MAKES 1 SERVING

NOTE: To broil, preheat broiler. Broil burger 4 to 6 inches from heat 6 minutes per side or until cooked through (165°F).

1-2-3 TUNA SALAD

1 can (6 ounces) solid white
   tuna packed in water,
   drained and flaked

2 tablespoons Caesar
   dressing

½ cup chopped celery

   Salt and black pepper

Combine tuna, dressing and celery in medium bowl; toss to coat. Season with salt and pepper.

MAKES 2 SERVINGS

EXTRAS: Serve this salad with toasted bread, grapes and romaine lettuce for a hearty main dish meal.

SWEET TUNA SALAD SANDWICHES

1 can (5 ounces) white tuna
   packed in water, drained

1½ tablespoons mayonnaise

½ cup chopped unpeeled
   apple

2 leaves red leaf or romaine
   lettuce

4 slices whole grain
   cinnamon-raisin swirl
   bread, lightly toasted

Combine tuna and mayonnaise in medium bowl; mix well. Stir in apple. Arrange lettuce over 2 slices toast; top with tuna mixture. Close sandwiches with remaining toast; cut in half diagonally.

MAKES 2 SERVINGS

VARIATION: Prepare open-faced sandwiches by using only 1 slice of toast.

78

VEGETARIAN FAVORITES

CHARRED CORN SALAD

3 tablespoons fresh lime juice

½ teaspoon salt

¼ cup extra virgin olive oil

4 to 6 ears corn, husked (enough to make 3 to 4 cups kernels)

⅔ cup canned black beans, rinsed and drained

½ cup chopped fresh cilantro

2 teaspoons minced seeded chipotle pepper *or* 1 canned chipotle pepper in adobo sauce*

Chipotle peppers can sting and irritate the skin, so wear rubber gloves when handling peppers and do not touch your eyes.

1. Whisk lime juice and salt in small bowl. Gradually whisk in oil until well blended. Set aside.

2. Cut corn kernels off cobs. Heat large skillet over medium-high heat. Cook corn in single layer 15 to 17 minutes or until browned and tender, turning frequently. Transfer to large plate to cool slightly. Place in medium bowl.

3. Place beans in small microwavable bowl; microwave on HIGH 1 minute or until heated through. Add beans, cilantro and chipotle pepper to corn; mix well. Pour lime juice mixture over corn mixture; stir to coat.

MAKES 6 SERVINGS

NOTE: Chipotle peppers in adobo sauce are available canned in the Mexican food section of most supermarkets. Since only a small amount is needed for this dish, spoon leftovers into a covered food storage container and refrigerate or freeze.

SWEET POTATOES WITH CRANBERRY-GINGER GLAZE

2 medium sweet potatoes

½ cup dried cranberries

¼ cup cranberry juice

¼ cup maple syrup

2 slices (⅛ inch thick) fresh ginger

Dash black pepper

1. Pierce potatoes all over with fork. Microwave on HIGH 10 minutes or until soft. Peel and cut potatoes into wedges; place in serving dish.

2. Meanwhile, for glaze, place cranberries, juice, syrup, ginger and pepper in small saucepan. Cook over low heat 7 to 10 minutes or until syrupy. Discard ginger. Pour glaze over potatoes.

MAKES 4 SERVINGS

BRAISED BRUSSELS SPROUTS WITH CARAMELIZED ONIONS

½ tablespoon butter

1 cup diced onion

5 tablespoons cola beverage, divided

1 teaspoon balsamic vinegar

1 pound Brussels sprouts, trimmed and halved lengthwise

3 tablespoons dry white wine, divided

Salt and black pepper

1. Heat butter in large skillet over medium heat. Reduce heat to medium-low and add onion; cook 10 minutes. Add 1 tablespoon cola and vinegar; cook 5 minutes.

2. Cook Brussels sprouts in boiling water, in medium saucepan about 5 minutes; drain. Add Brussels sprouts to skillet with onion and increase heat to medium. Add 2 tablespoons wine and 2 tablespoons cola; cook about 3 minutes or until most liquid has evaporated from skillet.

3. Add remaining 1 tablespoon wine and 2 tablespoons cola to skillet; stir and cook 2 minutes or until most liquid has evaporated from skillet and Brussels sprouts are tender. Season with salt and pepper.

MAKES 4 SERVINGS

NOTE: The caramelized onions add a tasty touch to these bright green vegetables.

SAVORY STUFFED TOMATOES

2 large ripe tomatoes
(1 to 1¼ pounds total)

¾ cup garlic- or Caesar-
flavored croutons

¼ cup chopped pitted
kalamata olives

2 tablespoons chopped
fresh basil

1 clove garlic, minced

2 tablespoons grated
Parmesan or Romano
cheese

1 tablespoon olive oil

1. Preheat oven to 425°F. Cut tomatoes in half crosswise; discard seeds. Scrape out and reserve pulp. Place tomato shells cut side up in pie plate or pan; set aside.

2. Chop up tomato pulp; place in medium bowl. Add croutons, olives, basil and garlic; toss well. Spoon mixture into tomato shells. Sprinkle with cheese and drizzle oil over shells. Bake about 10 minutes or until heated through.

MAKES 4 SERVINGS

PENNE PASTA WITH CHUNKY TOMATO SAUCE AND SPINACH

8 ounces uncooked multigrain penne pasta

2 cups spicy marinara sauce

1 large ripe tomato, chopped (about 1½ cups)

4 cups packed baby spinach or torn spinach leaves (4 ounces)

¼ cup grated Parmesan cheese

¼ cup chopped fresh basil

1. Cook pasta according to package directions, omitting salt.

2. Meanwhile, heat marinara sauce and tomato in medium saucepan over medium heat 3 to 4 minutes or until hot and bubbly, stirring occasionally. Remove from heat; stir in spinach.

3. Drain pasta; return to saucepan. Add sauce; toss to combine. Divide evenly among eight serving bowls; top with cheese and basil.

MAKES 8 (¾ CUP) SERVINGS

BARBECUE TOFU

1 package (14 ounces) extra firm tofu

1 bottle (18 ounces) barbecue sauce

4 to 6 pieces frozen Texas toast, prepared according to package directions

Prepared coleslaw

1. Place tofu on paper towel-lined plate; cover with another paper towel. Place weighted saucepan or baking dish on top of tofu. Let stand 15 minutes to drain. Cut tofu into eight equal slices.

2. Spread half of barbecue sauce in large saucepan; arrange tofu slices over sauce in single layer. Top with remaining sauce. Cover; cook over medium heat 5 minutes. Turn tofu. Cover; cook 5 minutes or until heated through.

3. Serve tofu over Texas toast. Drizzle with sauce; serve with coleslaw.

MAKES 4 TO 6 SERVINGS

STIR-FRY VEGETABLE PIZZA

1 pound (about 5 cups) fresh cut stir-fry vegetables (packaged or from the salad bar) such as broccoli, zucchini, bell peppers and red onions

1 (12-inch) prepared pizza crust

⅓ cup pizza sauce

¼ teaspoon red pepper flakes (optional)

1½ cups (6 ounces) shredded part-skim mozzarella cheese

1. Heat oven to 425°F.

2. Heat large skillet over medium-high heat 1 minute; coat with nonstick cooking spray. Add vegetables; stir-fry 4 to 5 minutes or until crisp-tender.

3. Place pizza crust on large baking sheet; top with pizza sauce. Sprinkle red pepper flakes over sauce, if desired. Arrange vegetables over sauce; top with cheese.

4. Bake 12 to 14 minutes or until crust is golden brown and cheese is melted. Cut into eight wedges.

MAKES 4 SERVINGS

RANCHERO MACARONI BAKE

1   can (26 ounces)
     CAMPBELL'S® Condensed
     Cream of Mushroom Soup
     (Regular **or** 98% Fat Free)

1   cup milk

1   cup PACE® Picante Sauce

3   cups shredded Cheddar
     cheese **or** Monterey Jack
     cheese

3   cups elbow macaroni,
     cooked and drained

1   cup coarsely crushed
     tortilla chips

1. Stir the soup, milk, picante sauce, cheese and macaroni in a 3-quart shallow baking dish.

2. Bake at 400°F. for 20 minutes or until the macaroni mixture is hot and bubbling. Stir the macaroni mixture. Sprinkle with the tortilla chips.

3. Bake for 5 minutes or until the tortilla chips are golden brown.

MAKES 8 SERVINGS

MINESTRONE SOUP

¾ cup uncooked small shell pasta

2 cans (about 14 ounces each) vegetable broth

1 can (28 ounces) crushed tomatoes in tomato purée

1 can (about 15 ounces) white beans, rinsed and drained

1 package (16 ounces) frozen vegetable medley, such as broccoli, green beans, carrots and red peppers

4 to 6 teaspoons prepared pesto

1. Cook pasta according to package directions; drain.

2. Meanwhile, combine broth, tomatoes and beans in large saucepan; bring to a boil over high heat. Reduce heat to low; cover and simmer 3 to 5 minutes.

3. Add vegetables to broth mixture; return to a boil over high heat. Stir in pasta; simmer, uncovered, until vegetables and pasta are tender. Ladle soup into bowls; top each serving with about 1 teaspoon pesto.

MAKES 4 TO 6 SERVINGS

BLACK BEAN & RICE STUFFED POBLANO PEPPERS

2 large or 4 small poblano peppers

½ of a 15-ounce can black beans, rinsed and drained

½ cup cooked brown rice

⅓ cup mild or medium chunky salsa

⅓ cup shredded Cheddar cheese or pepper Jack cheese, divided

1. Preheat oven to 375°F. Lightly spray shallow baking pan with nonstick olive oil cooking spray.

2. Cut thin slice from one side of each pepper. Chop pepper slices; set aside. In medium saucepan, cook remaining peppers in boiling water 6 minutes. Drain and rinse with cold water. Remove and discard seeds and membranes.

3. Stir together beans, rice, salsa, chopped pepper and ¼ cup cheese in small bowl. Spoon into peppers, mounding mixture. Place peppers in prepared pan. Cover with foil. Bake 12 to 15 minutes or until heated through.

4. Sprinkle with remaining cheese. Bake 2 minutes or until cheese is melted.

MAKES 2 SERVINGS

SHELLS AND GORGONZOLA

1 pound uncooked medium shell pasta

1 jar (24 ounces) vodka sauce

1 package (4 ounces) crumbled Gorgonzola cheese

Chopped fresh rosemary (optional)

1. Cook pasta according to package directions. Drain well; cover and keep warm.

2. Meanwhile, heat sauce in medium saucepan over medium heat.

3. Toss pasta with sauce until well blended. Top with cheese just before serving. Garnish with rosemary.

MAKES 4 TO 6 SERVINGS

VARIATION: Add 2 cups packed torn spinach to the hot drained pasta; continue as directed above.

BALSAMIC BUTTERNUT SQUASH

3 tablespoons olive oil

2 tablespoons thinly sliced fresh sage (about 6 large leaves), divided

1 medium butternut squash, peeled and cut into 1-inch pieces (4 to 5 cups)

½ red onion, cut in half and cut into ¼-inch slices

1 teaspoon salt, divided

2½ tablespoons balsamic vinegar

¼ teaspoon black pepper

1. Heat oil in large (12-inch) cast iron skillet over medium-high heat. Add 1 tablespoon sage; cook and stir 3 minutes. Add squash, onion and ½ teaspoon salt; cook 6 minutes, stirring occasionally. Reduce heat to medium; cook 15 minutes without stirring.

2. Stir in vinegar, remaining ½ teaspoon salt and pepper; cook 10 minutes or until squash is tender, stirring occasionally. Stir in remaining 1 tablespoon sage; cook 1 minute.

MAKES 4 SERVINGS

SPAGHETTI WITH PESTO TOFU SQUARES

1 package (14 ounces) extra firm tofu

¼ to ½ cup prepared pesto

½ of a 16-ounce package uncooked spaghetti

1 jar (24 ounces) marinara sauce

½ cup shredded Parmesan cheese

¼ cup pine nuts, toasted*

To toast nuts, spread in shallow baking pan. Bake in preheated 350°F oven 5 to 7 minutes or until golden, stirring frequently.

1. Preheat oven to 350°F. Spray shallow baking dish with nonstick cooking spray.

2. Cut tofu into 1-inch cubes. Combine tofu and pesto in medium bowl; toss to coat. Arrange in prepared baking dish. Bake 15 minutes.

3. Meanwhile, cook spaghetti according to package directions; drain and return to saucepan. Add marinara sauce; toss to coat. Cover; cook 5 minutes over low heat or until heated through.

4. Divide spaghetti among four plates; top with tofu cubes. Sprinkle with cheese and pine nuts.

MAKES 4 SERVINGS

ROASTED TACO CAULIFLOWER

1   head cauliflower, cut into florets

2   tablespoons olive oil

1   packet (1.25 ounces) ORTEGA® Taco Seasoning Mix or 40% Less Sodium Taco Seasoning Mix

PREHEAT oven to 425°F.

PLACE cauliflower on large rimmed baking sheet. Drizzle oil over cauliflower and sprinkle with seasoning mix; toss to coat evenly.

BAKE 25 minutes or until cauliflower is tender. Serve warm.

MAKES 4 TO 6 SERVINGS

TIP: ORTEGA® Taco Seasoning Mix also adds great flavor to other roasted vegetables, such as carrots, turnips or Brussels sprouts. Prepare as directed.

BASIL PESTO ALFREDO PIZZA

1 package (16 ounces) cooked pizza crust (**two** 11-inch crusts)

1 jar (14.5 ounces) PREGO® Basil Pesto Alfredo Sauce

1 cup shredded mozzarella cheese (about 4 ounces)

2 medium tomatoes, cut into ¼-inch slices

¼ cup sliced fresh basil leaves

1. Heat the oven to 425°F.

2. Place the pizza crusts onto **2** baking sheets. Spread **about ¾ cup** alfredo sauce over **each** crust to within ½-inch of the edge. Sprinkle with the cheese and top with the tomato slices. Season the tomatoes as desired.

3. Bake for 12 minutes or until the cheese is melted. Sprinkle with the basil. Let stand for 5 minutes and cut **each** pizza into 6 slices.

MAKES 12 SERVINGS

PICKLED JALAPEÑO BLACK BEAN SKILLET

¾ cup instant white rice

1 can (about 15 ounces) black beans, rinsed and drained

½ to 1 ounce pickled jalapeño peppers,* chopped

¼ teaspoon salt

½ cup (2 ounces) shredded Mexican cheese

¼ cup chopped fresh cilantro

½ cup sour cream

Jalapeño peppers can sting and irritate the skin, so wear rubber gloves when handling peppers and do not touch your eyes.

1. Cook rice according to package directions, omitting any salt or fat. Remove from heat.

2. Stir beans, jalapeño peppers and salt into rice. Sprinkle evenly with cheese. Cover; cook 5 minutes over medium-low heat or until cheese is melted. Serve topped with cilantro and sour cream.

MAKES 4 SERVINGS

ITALIAN BEANS AND GREENS SOUP IN A MUG

¼ cup canned diced tomatoes with basil, garlic and oregano, drained

1 teaspoon olive oil

¼ teaspoon minced garlic

⅛ teaspoon black pepper

¼ cup finely chopped kale or spinach

¼ cup cannellini beans, rinsed and drained

1 cup vegetable broth

MICROWAVE DIRECTIONS

1. Combine tomatoes, oil, garlic and pepper in large microwavable mug; mix well. Microwave on HIGH 1 minute; stir.

2. Add kale and beans to mug; pour in broth. Microwave on HIGH 3 minutes or until heated through. Let stand, covered, 2 to 3 minutes before serving.

MAKES 1 SERVING

BEEF & PORK

CUMIN-RUBBED STEAKS WITH AVOCADO SALSA VERDE

2 beef shoulder center steaks (ranch), cut 1 inch thick (about 8 ounces *each*)

2 teaspoons ground cumin

¾ cup prepared tomatillo salsa

1 small avocado, diced

2 tablespoons chopped fresh cilantro

1. Press cumin evenly onto beef steaks. Heat large nonstick skillet over medium heat until hot. Place steaks in skillet; cook 13 to 16 minutes for medium rare (145°F) to medium (160°F) doneness, turning occasionally.

2. Meanwhile, combine salsa, avocado and cilantro in small bowl.

3. Carve steaks into slices; season with salt, as desired. Serve with salsa.

MAKES 4 SERVINGS

TIP: Two beef top loin (strip) steaks, cut 1 inch thick, may be substituted for shoulder center steaks. Cook 12 to 15 minutes, turning occasionally.

Courtesy of The Beef Checkoff

TERIYAKI RIB DINNER

1 package (about 15 ounces) refrigerated fully cooked pork baby back ribs in barbecue sauce

2 tablespoons vegetable oil

1 large onion, thinly sliced

4 cups frozen stir-fry vegetables

1 can (8 ounces) pineapple chunks, undrained *or* 1 cup diced fresh pineapple

¼ cup hoisin sauce

2 tablespoons cider vinegar

1. Remove ribs from package; reserve barbecue sauce. Cut into individual ribs; set aside.

2. Heat oil in Dutch oven over medium-high heat. Add onion; cook 3 minutes or until translucent. Add vegetables; cook and stir 4 minutes.

3. Add ribs, reserved sauce, pineapple, hoisin sauce and vinegar; mix well. Cover; cook 5 minutes or until heated through.

MAKES 4 SERVINGS

QUICK & EASY MEATBALL SOUP

1 package (15 to 18 ounces) frozen Italian sausage meatballs without sauce

2 cans (about 14 ounces each) Italian-style stewed tomatoes

2 cans (about 14 ounces each) beef broth

1 can (about 14 ounces) mixed vegetables

½ cup uncooked rotini pasta or small macaroni

½ teaspoon dried oregano

1. Thaw meatballs in microwave according to package directions.

2. Place tomatoes, broth, mixed vegetables, pasta and oregano in large saucepan. Add meatballs; bring to a boil over medium-high heat. Reduce heat to medium-low. Simmer, covered, 15 minutes or until pasta is tender.

MAKES 4 TO 6 SERVINGS

MAC AND CHEESE TOSS

8 ounces ham, diced

4 cups (1 quart) prepared deli macaroni and cheese

½ cup frozen green peas, thawed

¼ cup milk

MICROWAVE DIRECTIONS

1. Combine ham, macaroni and cheese, peas and milk in microwavable 2-quart casserole; toss gently to blend.

2. Microwave, covered, on HIGH 3 minutes; stir. Microwave 1 minute or until heated through.

MAKES 4 SERVINGS

NOTE: To thaw peas quickly, place them in a small colander under cold running water 15 to 20 seconds or until thawed. Drain liquid.

TACO-TOPPED BAKED POTATOES

- 4 large baking potatoes, scrubbed
- ½ pound (8 ounces) lean ground beef
- ¼ cup chopped onion
- 1 packet (1.25 ounces) ORTEGA® Taco Seasoning Mix
- 1 container (13 ounces) ORTEGA® Salsa & Cheese Bowl

  Salt, to taste

  Sour cream (optional)

PRICK potatoes several times with a fork. Microwave on HIGH (100%) uncovered, 12 to 15 minutes or until just tender, turning potatoes over and re-arranging once.

CRUMBLE ground beef into 1-quart glass casserole; add onion. Microwave on HIGH (100%) uncovered, 3 to 3½ minutes or until meat is set, stirring once; drain.

STIR in taco seasoning and half the amount of water specified on taco seasoning package. Add contents of Salsa & Cheese Bowl. Cover; microwave on HIGH (100%) 2½ to 3 minutes or until heated through, stirring once.

MAKE a crosswise slash in each potato; press side of potato to form an opening. Sprinkle with salt. Spoon filling into potatoes.

TOP each potato with sour cream, if desired.

MAKES 4 SERVINGS

PORK & ASPARAGUS STIR-FRY

1 cup uncooked rice

¾ pound pork tenderloin

3 tablespoons Chinese black bean sauce

½ teaspoon black pepper

¾ pound asparagus (25 to 30 spears)

2 to 3 tablespoons water

1. Cook rice according to package directions. Keep warm.

2. Trim pork and cut into bite-size pieces. Heat large nonstick skillet or wok over medium-high heat. Add pork, black bean sauce and pepper; stir-fry 5 minutes or until pork is browned.

3. Cut asparagus into bite-size pieces. Add asparagus and water to skillet; stir-fry 7 minutes or until pork is cooked through and asparagus is crisp-tender, adding additional water if needed to prevent sticking. Serve over rice.

MAKES 4 SERVINGS

EXTRAS: Add red or green bell pepper strips with the asparagus and/or serve over noodles instead of rice. Garnish with chopped green onions.

BEEF CHILI FIVE WAYS

1 pound Ground Beef (93% lean or leaner)

1 can (15½ ounces) black beans, rinsed and drained

1 can (14 to 14½-ounces) reduced-sodium or regular beef broth

1 can (14½ ounces) diced tomatoes with green chiles

2 tablespoons chili powder

TOPPINGS:

Shredded Cheddar cheese, chopped fresh cilantro, minced green onion (optional)

1. Heat large nonstick skillet over medium heat until hot. Add Ground Beef; cook 8 to 10 minutes, breaking into ¾-inch crumbles and stirring occasionally. Pour off drippings.

2. Stir in beans, broth, tomatoes and chili powder; bring to a boil. Reduce heat. Cover and simmer 20 minutes to develop flavors, stirring occasionally. Garnish with Toppings, as desired.

MAKES 4 SERVINGS

Courtesy of The Beef Checkoff

MOROCCAN CHILI: Prepare recipe as directed above, adding ¼ teaspoon pumpkin pie spice and ¼ cup chopped pitted dates or golden raisins with ingredients in step 2. Serve over hot cooked couscous. Garnish with toasted sliced almonds, chopped fresh mint and Greek yogurt, as desired.

MEXICAN CHILI: Prepare recipe as directed above, adding 1 tablespoon cocoa powder with ingredients in step 2. Garnish with chopped fresh cilantro, pepitas (pumpkin seeds) and corn tortilla chips, as desired. Serve with corn tortillas.

ITALIAN CHILI: Prepare recipe as directed above, adding 1½ teaspoons fennel seed with ingredients in step 2. Before removing from heat, stir in 3 cups fresh baby spinach. Cover; turn off heat and let stand 3 to 5 minutes or until spinach is just wilted. Serve over hot cooked orecchiette or cavatappi, if desired. Garnish with grated Parmesan cheese and pine nuts, as desired.

CINCINNATI CHILI: Prepare recipe as directed above, adding 3 tablespoons white vinegar and 1 teaspoon ground cinnamon with ingredients in step 2. Serve over hot cooked elbow macaroni. Garnish with chopped white onion, sour cream and shredded Cheddar cheese, as desired.

SMOTHERED PORK CHOPS

2 tablespoons cornstarch

1¾ cups SWANSON® Beef
   Stock

¼ teaspoon ground black
   pepper

   Vegetable cooking spray

6 bone-in pork chops, ½-inch
   thick (about 1½ pounds)

1 large onion, sliced (about
   1 cup)

1. Stir the cornstarch, stock and black pepper in a small bowl until the mixture is smooth.

2. Spray a 12-inch skillet with the cooking spray and heat over medium-high heat for 1 minute. Add the pork and cook for 5 minutes or until it's well browned on both sides. Remove the pork from the skillet. Remove the skillet from the heat.

3. Reduce the heat to medium. Spray the skillet with the cooking spray and heat for 1 minute. Add the onion and cook until it's tender-crisp, stirring occasionally.

4. Stir the stock mixture in the skillet. Cook and stir until the mixture boils and thickens. Return the pork to the skillet. Reduce the heat to low. Cover and cook for 5 minutes or until the pork is cooked through.

MAKES 6 SERVINGS

ORIENTAL BEEF WITH VEGETABLES

1 pound ground beef

1 large onion, coarsely chopped

2 cloves garlic, minced

2½ cups (8 ounces) frozen mixed vegetable medley, such as carrots, broccoli and red peppers, thawed

½ cup stir-fry sauce

1 can (3 ounces) chow mein noodles

1. Cook beef and onion in large skillet over medium-high heat 6 to 8 minutes or until beef is no longer pink, stirring to break up meat. Drain fat.

2. Add garlic; stir-fry 1 minute. Add vegetables; stir-fry 2 minutes or until heated through.

3. Add stir-fry sauce; stir-fry 30 seconds or until heated through. Serve over chow mein noodles.

MAKES 4 SERVINGS

GARLIC BEEF

1 teaspoon sesame oil

1 pound beef eye of round, trimmed, cut into thin strips

1 package (10 ounces) frozen chopped broccoli

1 tablespoon minced garlic

1 tablespoon soy sauce

¼ teaspoon black pepper

Heat oil in large skillet over high heat. Add beef, broccoli, garlic, soy sauce and pepper. Cook, stirring occasionally, 15 minutes or until beef is done.

MAKES 4 SERVINGS

MINI PIZZAS

½ cup PREGO® Italian Sausage & Garlic Italian Sauce

4 slices Italian bread, ½-inch thick, toasted

1 ounce shredded mozzarella cheese (about ¼ cup)

1. Spread **about 2 tablespoons** Italian sauce on **each** bread slice. Top with the cheese. Place the pizzas on a microwavable plate.

2. Microwave on HIGH for 1 minute or until the cheese is melted.

MAKES 2 SERVINGS

ROAST BEEF ROLL-UPS

2 tablespoons horseradish mayonnaise

2 thin slices roast beef (1 ounce)

¼ cup (1 ounce) crumbled blue cheese

1 ounce sliced red onion

1. Spread mayonnaise on roast beef slice. Sprinkle with blue cheese; layer with onion slices.

2. Roll up roast beef slice from short ends.

MAKES 2 SERVINGS

ALL-IN-ONE BURGER STEW

1 pound ground beef

2 cups frozen Italian-style
vegetables

1 can (about 14 ounces)
diced tomatoes with
basil and garlic

1 can (about 14 ounces) beef
broth

2½ cups uncooked medium
egg noodles

Salt and black pepper

1. Brown beef in Dutch oven or large skillet 6 to
8 minutes over medium-high heat, stirring to
break up meat. Drain fat.

2. Add vegetables, tomatoes and broth; bring
to a boil over high heat.

3. Add noodles; reduce heat to medium. Cover;
cook 12 to 15 minutes or until vegetables and
noodles are tender. Season with salt and
pepper.

MAKES 6 SERVINGS

NOTE: For a special touch, sprinkle with chopped
parsley before serving.

TIP: To complete this meal, serve with breadsticks
or a loaf of Italian bread and a simple salad.

TASTY 2-STEP PORK CHOPS

1 tablespoon vegetable oil

4 bone-in pork chops, ½-inch thick (about 1½ pounds)

1 can CAMPBELL'S® Condensed Cream of Mushroom Soup **or** CAMPBELL'S® Condensed 98% Fat Free Cream of Mushroom Soup

½ cup water

1. Heat the oil in a 10-inch skillet over medium-high heat. Add the pork and cook until well browned on both sides.

2. Stir the soup and water in the skillet and heat to a boil. Reduce the heat to low. Cover and cook for 10 minutes or until the pork is cooked through.

MAKES 4 SERVINGS

TIP: Also great with CAMPBELL'S® Condensed Cream of Mushroom with Roasted Garlic Soup, with ½ cup milk instead of water.

SKILLET MAC & BEEF

1   pound ground beef

1   medium onion, chopped
    (about ½ cup)

1   can (10½ ounces)
    CAMPBELL'S® Condensed
    Cream of Celery Soup **or**
    CAMPBELL'S® Condensed
    98% Fat Free Cream of
    Celery Soup

¼   cup ketchup

1   tablespoon Worcestershire
    sauce

8   ounces (about 2 cups) rotini
    (spiral) pasta, cooked
    and drained

1. Cook the beef and onion in a 10-inch skillet over medium-high heat until the beef is well browned, stirring frequently to separate the meat. Pour off any fat.

2. Stir the soup, ketchup, Worcestershire and rotini into the skillet and heat through. Reduce the heat to medium. Cook until the mixture is hot and bubbling, stirring occasionally.

MAKES 4 SERVINGS

STIR-FRY BEEF & VEGETABLE SOUP

1   boneless beef top sirloin
    or top round steak (about
    1 pound)

2   teaspoons dark sesame oil,
    divided

3   cans (about 14 ounces
    each) beef broth

1   package (16 ounces) frozen
    stir-fry vegetables

3   green onions, thinly sliced

¼   cup stir-fry sauce

1. Slice beef lengthwise in half, then crosswise into ⅛-inch-thick strips.

2. Heat 1 teaspoon sesame oil in large saucepan or Dutch oven over medium-high heat; tilt pan to coat bottom. Add half of beef in single layer. Cook 1 minute, without stirring, until lightly browned on bottom. Turn and cook other side about 1 minute. Remove beef from saucepan. Repeat with remaining 1 teaspoon sesame oil and beef; set aside.

3. Add broth to saucepan. Cover; bring to a boil over high heat. Add vegetables. Reduce heat; simmer 3 to 5 minutes or until vegetables are heated through. Add beef, green onions and stir-fry sauce; simmer 1 minute.

MAKES 6 SERVINGS

SERVING SUGGESTION: Make a quick sesame bread to serve with this soup. Brush refrigerated dinner roll dough with water, then dip in sesame seeds before baking.

BRATWURST SKILLET

1   pound bratwurst links, cut into ½-inch slices

1½ cups sliced onions

1½ cups green bell pepper strips

1½ cups red bell pepper strips

1   teaspoon paprika

1   teaspoon caraway seeds

1. Heat large skillet over medium heat. Add bratwurst; cover and cook 5 minutes or until browned and no longer pink in center. Transfer bratwurst to plate. Cover and keep warm.

2. Drain all but 1 tablespoon drippings from skillet. Add onions, bell peppers, paprika and caraway seeds. Cook and stir about 5 minutes or until vegetables are tender.

3. Combine bratwurst and vegetables. Serve immediately.

MAKES 4 SERVINGS

SERVING SUGGESTION: Top with cherry tomato halves and celery leaves.

TIP: To make this even speedier, purchase a packaged stir-fry pepper and onion mix and use in place of the fresh bell peppers and onions.

CHEESEBURGER CALZONES

1 pound ground beef

1 medium onion, chopped

½ teaspoon salt

1 jar (1 pound 8 ounces) RAGÚ® Chunky Pasta Sauce

1 jar (8 ounces) marinated mushrooms, drained and chopped (optional)

1 cup shredded Cheddar cheese (about 4 ounces)

1 package (12 ounces) refrigerated large flaky biscuits (8 biscuits)

1. Preheat oven to 375°F. In 12-inch skillet, brown ground beef with onion and salt over medium-high heat; drain. Stir in 1 cup Pasta Sauce, mushrooms and cheese.

2. Roll or press out each biscuit to a 6-inch circle. Place ½ cup beef mixture on each dough circle; fold over and press edges to close. Seal completely by pressing firmly along edges with the tines of a fork.

3. With large spatula, gently arrange on cookie sheets. Bake 13 minutes or until golden. Serve with remaining sauce, heated.

MAKES 8 SERVINGS

BEEFY ENCHILADA SKILLET

1 pound ground beef

1 jar (16 ounces) PACE®
  Picante Sauce-Medium
  or PACE® Chunky Salsa-
  Mild

8 corn tortillas (6-inch), cut
  into 1-inch squares

1 cup shredded Cheddar
  cheese (about 4 ounces)

¼ cup sour cream (optional)

1 tablespoon chopped green
  onion (optional)

1. Cook the beef in a 10-inch skillet over medium-high heat until it's well browned, stirring often to separate meat. Pour off any fat.

2. Stir the picante sauce, tortillas and **half** of the cheese in the skillet and heat to a boil. Reduce the heat to low. Cover and cook for 5 minutes or until the beef mixture is hot and bubbling.

3. Top with the remaining cheese. Serve with the sour cream and green onion, if desired.

MAKES 4 SERVINGS

BEEF TERIYAKI STIR-FRY

1 cup uncooked rice

1 boneless beef top sirloin steak (about 1 pound)

½ cup teriyaki sauce, divided

2 tablespoons vegetable oil, divided

1 medium onion, halved and sliced

2 cups frozen green beans, thawed

1. Cook rice according to package directions. Keep warm.

2. Cut beef lengthwise in half, then crosswise into ⅛-inch slices. Combine beef and ¼ cup teriyaki sauce in medium bowl; set aside.

3. Heat 1½ teaspoons oil in large skillet or wok over medium-high heat. Add onion; stir-fry 3 to 4 minutes or until crisp-tender. Remove from skillet to another medium bowl.

4. Heat 1½ teaspoons oil in skillet. Stir-fry green beans 3 minutes or until crisp-tender and heated through. Drain excess liquid. Add beans to onion in bowl.

5. Heat remaining 1 tablespoon oil in skillet. Drain beef, discarding marinade. Stir-fry half of beef 2 minutes or until barely pink in center. Add to vegetables. Repeat with remaining beef. Return beef mixture to skillet. Stir in remaining ¼ cup teriyaki sauce; cook and stir 1 minute or until heated through. Serve with rice.

MAKES 4 SERVINGS

SPEEDY CHICKEN

GRILLED BUFFALO CHICKEN WRAPS

4 boneless skinless chicken breasts (about 4 ounces each)

¼ cup plus 2 tablespoons buffalo wing sauce, divided

2 cups broccoli slaw

1 tablespoon blue cheese salad dressing

4 (8-inch) whole wheat tortillas, warmed

1. Place chicken in large resealable food storage bag. Add ¼ cup buffalo sauce; seal bag. Marinate in refrigerator 15 minutes.

2. Meanwhile, prepare grill for direct cooking over medium-high heat. Grill chicken 5 to 6 minutes per side or until no longer pink. When cool enough to handle, slice chicken and combine with remaining 2 tablespoons buffalo sauce in medium bowl.

3. Combine broccoli slaw and blue cheese dressing in medium bowl; mix well.

4. Arrange chicken and broccoli slaw evenly down center of each tortilla. Roll up to secure filling. To serve, cut in half diagonally.

MAKES 4 SERVINGS

VARIATION: If you don't like the spicy flavor of buffalo wing sauce, substitute your favorite barbecue sauce.

ITALIAN CHICKEN & PEPPERS

6 cups hot cooked spaghetti **or** whole grain spaghetti (from about 12 ounces dry)

1¾ pounds skinless, boneless chicken breast halves **and**/**or** thighs, cut into 1-inch cubes

1 tablespoon vegetable oil

2 medium green peppers, cut into 2-inch-long strips (about 3 cups) (any color bell pepper will work in this recipe)

2 large onions, chopped (about 2 cups)

2 cloves garlic, minced **or** ½ teaspoon garlic powder

1 jar (24 ounces) PREGO® Traditional Italian Sauce

1. While the spaghetti is cooking, season the chicken as desired. Heat the oil in a 12-inch skillet over medium-high heat. Add the chicken and cook until well browned, stirring often.

2. Reduce the heat to medium. Stir the peppers, onions and garlic in the skillet and cook until the chicken is cooked through and the vegetables are tender.

3. Stir in the sauce and cook until the mixture is hot and bubbling. Season to taste. Serve the chicken mixture over the spaghetti. Sprinkle with grated Parmesan cheese, if desired.

MAKES 6 SERVINGS

EASY SUBSTITUTION: You can substitute Italian pork sausage, cut into 1-inch pieces, for the chicken. Omit the oil and brown the sausage as directed in Step 1. Pour off all but 1 tablespoon drippings from the skillet and proceed as shown above in Step 2.

2-STEP SKILLET CHICKEN BROCCOLI DIVAN

1 tablespoon butter

1¼ pounds skinless, boneless chicken breast halves, cut into 1-inch pieces

3 cups fresh or frozen broccoli florets

1 can CAMPBELL'S® Condensed Cream of Chicken Soup **or** CAMPBELL'S® Condensed 98% Fat Free Cream of Chicken Soup

½ cup reduced fat (2%) milk

½ cup shredded Cheddar cheese

1. Heat the butter in a 10-inch skillet over medium-high heat. Add the chicken and cook until well browned, stirring often.

2. Stir the broccoli, soup and milk in the skillet. Reduce the heat to low. Cover and cook for 5 minutes or until the chicken is cooked through. Sprinkle with the cheese.

MAKES 4 SERVINGS

FLAVOR VARIATION: Try this recipe with CAMPBELL'S® Condensed Cream of Mushroom Soup and shredded Swiss cheese.

QUICK CHICKEN TACOS

1   can (4.5 ounces) SWANSON®
    Premium White Chunk
    Chicken Breast in Water,
    drained

¼   cup PACE® Salsa

    Shredded lettuce

4   taco shells

    Shredded Cheddar cheese

    Sour cream

1. Stir the chicken and salsa in a 1-quart saucepan. Heat over low heat until the mixture is hot and bubbling, stirring often.

2. Arrange the lettuce in the taco shells. Top with **¼ cup** chicken mixture, cheese and sour cream. Serve with additional salsa, if desired.

MAKES 2 SERVINGS

SIZZLING FAJITAS

2   tablespoons vegetable oil

1   pound skinless, boneless
    chicken breast halves **or**
    beef sirloin steak, cut into
    strips

1   medium green **or** red
    pepper, cut into 2-inch-
    long strips (about 1½
    cups)

1   medium onion, sliced (about
    ½ cup)

1½ cups PACE® Picante Sauce

8   flour tortillas (8-inch),
    warmed

    Guacamole (optional)

1. Heat the oil in a 12-inch skillet over medium-high heat. Add the chicken and cook until well browned, stirring often.

2. Stir the pepper and onion in the skillet and cook until tender-crisp. Stir the picante sauce in the skillet and cook until the mixture is hot and bubbling.

3. Spoon **about ½ cup** chicken mixture down the center of **each** tortilla. Top with additional picante sauce. Fold the tortillas around the filling. Serve with the guacamole, if desired.

MAKES 4 SERVINGS

BEER OVEN-FRIED CHICKEN

1⅓ cups light-colored beer, such as pale ale

2 tablespoons buttermilk

1¼ cups panko bread crumbs*

½ cup grated Parmesan cheese

4 chicken breast cutlets (about 1¼ pounds)

½ teaspoon salt

¼ teaspoon black pepper

Panko bread crumbs are Japanese bread crumbs that are much lighter and less dense than ones often used in America. Panko bread crumbs can be found in Asian markets or in the Asian foods section of your supermarket.

1. Preheat oven to 400°F. Line large baking sheet with foil.

2. Combine beer and buttermilk in shallow bowl. Combine panko and cheese in another shallow bowl.

3. Sprinkle chicken with salt and pepper. Dip in beer mixture; roll in panko mixture to coat. Place on prepared baking sheet.

4. Bake 25 to 30 minutes or until chicken is no longer pink in center.

MAKES 4 SERVINGS

TIP: To make a substitution for buttermilk, place 1 teaspoon lemon juice or distilled white vinegar in a measuring cup and add enough milk to measure 2 tablespoons. Stir and let the mixture stand at room temperature for 5 minutes. Discard leftover mixture.

CHICKEN AND ASPARAGUS STIR-FRY

1 cup uncooked rice

2 tablespoons vegetable oil

1 pound boneless skinless chicken breasts, cut into ½-inch-wide strips

2 medium red bell peppers, cut into thin strips

½ pound fresh asparagus,* cut diagonally into 1-inch pieces

½ cup stir-fry sauce

For stir-frying, select thin stalks of asparagus.

1. Cook rice according to package directions; keep warm.

2. Heat oil in wok or large skillet over medium-high heat. Stir-fry chicken 3 to 4 minutes or until cooked through.

3. Stir in bell peppers and asparagus; reduce heat to medium. Cover; cook 2 minutes or until vegetables are crisp-tender, stirring once or twice.

4. Stir in sauce; heat through. Serve with rice.

MAKES 4 SERVINGS

15-MINUTE CHICKEN AND BROCCOLI RISOTTO

1   tablespoon vegetable oil

1   small onion, chopped

2   packages (about 9 ounces each) ready-to-serve yellow rice

2   cups frozen chopped broccoli

1   package (about 6 ounces) refrigerated fully cooked chicken breast strips, cut into pieces

½   cup chicken broth

    Sliced almonds (optional)

1. Heat oil in large skillet over medium-high heat. Add onion; cook and stir 3 minutes or until translucent.

2. Knead rice in bag. Add rice, broccoli, chicken and broth to skillet. Cover; cook 6 to 8 minutes or until heated through, stirring occasionally. Garnish with almonds.

MAKES 4 SERVINGS

SERVING SUGGESTION: Top with toasted sliced almonds for a crunchier texture and added flavor.

EASY CHICKEN POT PIE

1   can CAMPBELL'S®
    Condensed Cream
    of Chicken Soup **or**
    CAMPBELL'S® Condensed
    98% Fat Free Cream of
    Chicken Soup

1   cup reduced fat (2%) milk

1   package (12 ounces)
    frozen mixed vegetables
    (carrots, green beans,
    corn, peas), thawed
    (about 2¼ cups)

1   cup cubed cooked chicken
    or turkey

1   egg

1   cup biscuit baking mix

1. Heat the oven to 400°F. Stir the soup, ½ cup milk, vegetables and chicken in a 9-inch pie plate.

2. Stir the remaining milk, egg and baking mix in a small bowl. Spread the batter over the chicken mixture.

3. Bake for 20 minutes or until the topping is golden brown.

MAKES 4 SERVINGS

SERVING SUGGESTION: Serve with a cucumber and tomato salad with your favorite vinaigrette. For dessert serve chocolate ice cream sprinkled with pecan halves and toasted coconut.

LEMON BROCCOLI CHICKEN

1 lemon

1 tablespoon vegetable oil

4 skinless, boneless chicken breast halves (about 1¼ pounds)

1 can (10¾ ounces) CAMPBELL'S® Condensed Cream of Broccoli Soup (Regular **or** 98% Fat Free)

¼ cup milk

⅛ teaspoon ground black pepper

1. Cut **4** thin slices of the lemon. Squeeze **2 teaspoons** juice from the remaining lemon.

2. Heat the oil in a 10-inch skillet over medium-high heat. Add the chicken and cook for 10 minutes or until well browned on both sides.

3. Stir the soup, milk, lemon juice and black pepper in the skillet and heat to a boil. Top the chicken with the lemon slices. Reduce the heat to low. Cover and cook for 5 minutes or until the chicken is cooked through.

MAKES 4 SERVINGS

SERVING SUGGESTION: Serve with steamed broccoli and seasoned long-grain rice. For dessert, serve frozen yogurt.

CHICKEN, BROCCOLI AND TOMATO PASTA

1 box (16 ounces) uncooked penne pasta

3 tablespoons olive oil

3 cups broccoli

2 packages (9 ounces each) Italian-seasoned chicken tenders

2 cups cherry tomatoes

2 cups fontina cheese

   Shredded Parmesan cheese (optional)

1. Prepare pasta according to package directions; reserving 1 cup pasta water.

2. Meanwhile, heat oil in large skillet. Add broccoli; cook 8 minutes or until tender. Add reserved pasta water and chicken; cook 5 minutes. Add tomatoes; cook 1 minute. Remove from heat. Stir in fontina cheese until slightly melted. Top with Parmesan cheese, if desired.

MAKES 6 SERVINGS

CREAMY CHICKEN AND RICE SOUP

2 cups water

2 cans (3 ounces each) chunk chicken, undrained

½ cup uncooked instant rice

1 package (2 ounces) white cream sauce mix

2 tablespoons chopped onion

¾ teaspoon chicken bouillon granules

¼ teaspoon white pepper

MICROWAVE DIRECTIONS

1. Combine water, chicken, rice, sauce mix, onion, bouillon granules and pepper in medium microwavable mug; mix well.

2. Microwave on HIGH 6 to 8 minutes or until heated through. Let stand, covered, 5 minutes. Stir before serving.

MAKES 1 SERVING

FAJITA-SEASONED GRILLED CHICKEN

2 boneless skinless chicken breasts (about 4 ounces each)

1 bunch green onions, ends trimmed

1 tablespoon olive oil

2 teaspoons fajita seasoning mix

1. Prepare grill for direct cooking.

2. Brush chicken and green onions with oil. Sprinkle both sides of chicken breasts with seasoning mix. Grill chicken and onions 6 to 8 minutes or until chicken is no longer pink in center.

3. Serve chicken with onions.

MAKES 2 SERVINGS

QUESADILLA GRANDE

2 (8-inch) flour tortillas

2 to 3 large fresh stemmed spinach leaves

2 to 3 slices (about 3 ounces) cooked boneless skinless chicken breast

2 tablespoons salsa

1 tablespoon chopped fresh cilantro

¼ cup (1 ounce) shredded Monterey Jack cheese

2 teaspoons butter or margarine (optional)

1. Place 1 tortilla in large nonstick skillet; cover tortilla with spinach leaves. Place chicken in single layer over spinach. Spoon salsa over chicken. Sprinkle with cilantro; top with cheese. Place remaining tortilla on top, pressing tortilla down so filling becomes compact.

2. Cook over medium heat 4 to 5 minutes or until bottom tortilla is lightly browned. Holding top tortilla in place, gently turn over. Continue cooking 4 minutes or until bottom tortilla is browned and cheese is melted. For a crispy finish, place butter in skillet to melt; lift quesadilla to let butter flow into center of skillet. Cook 30 seconds. Turn over; continue cooking 30 seconds. Cut in half to serve.

MAKES 1 SERVING

BBQ CHICKEN STROMBOLI

1 rotisserie-roasted chicken*
   (2 to 2¼ pounds)

⅓ cup barbecue sauce

1 package (about 14 ounces)
   refrigerated pizza dough

1 cup (4 ounces) shredded
   Cheddar cheese

⅓ cup sliced green onions,
   divided

*If desired, use 8 ounces roast
chicken breast from the deli,
chopped, instead of the 2 cups
shredded rotisserie chicken.

1. Remove and discard skin from chicken. Shred chicken with two forks; discard bones. (You should have about 4 cups shredded chicken.) Combine 2 cups chicken and barbecue sauce in medium bowl until well blended. Cover and refrigerate or freeze remaining chicken for another use.

2. Preheat oven to 400°F. Lightly spray baking sheet with nonstick cooking spray. Unroll pizza dough on baking sheet; pat into 12×9-inch rectangle.

3. Spread chicken mixture lengthwise down center of dough, leaving 2½ inches on each side. Sprinkle with cheese and ¼ cup green onions. Fold long sides of dough over filling; press edges to seal.

4. Sprinkle with remaining green onions. Bake 19 to 22 minutes or until golden brown. Let stand 10 minutes before slicing.

MAKES 6 SERVINGS

FRIED RICE

1 tablespoon vegetable oil

3 eggs, lightly beaten

1 can (14½ ounces) chicken broth

1 package (16 ounces) frozen stir-fry vegetables, thawed

2 tablespoons soy sauce

2 cups MINUTE® White Rice, uncooked

Heat oil in large nonstick skillet over medium heat. Add eggs; scramble until done. Remove from skillet; cover to keep warm.

Add broth, vegetables and soy sauce to skillet; bring to a boil. Stir in rice; cover. Remove from heat. Let stand 5 minutes.

Stir in scrambled eggs. Serve immediately.

MAKES 4 SERVINGS

QUICK CHICKEN PARMESAN

1¼ pounds skinless, boneless chicken breast halves

2 cups PREGO® Traditional Italian Sauce **or** PREGO® Fresh Mushroom Italian Sauce

½ cup shredded mozzarella cheese

2 tablespoons grated Parmesan cheese

8 ounces (½ of a 1-pound package) spaghetti, cooked and drained (about 4 cups)

1. Place the chicken in a 2-quart shallow baking dish. Top the chicken with the sauce. Sprinkle with the mozzarella cheese and Parmesan cheese.

2. Bake at 400°F. for 25 minutes or until the chicken is cooked through. Serve the chicken and sauce with the spaghetti.

MAKES 4 SERVINGS

SKILLET CHICKEN CREOLE

1   small red onion, chopped

1   small red bell pepper, chopped

1   jalapeño pepper,* seeded and minced

2   cups canned crushed tomatoes

¼   teaspoon salt (optional)

⅛   teaspoon black pepper

12   ounces boneless skinless chicken breasts, cut into strips

*Jalapeño peppers can sting and irritate the skin, so wear rubber gloves when handling peppers and do not touch your eyes.

1. Spray large nonstick skillet with nonstick cooking spray; heat over medium heat. Add onion, bell pepper and jalapeño pepper; cook over medium heat 5 to 10 minutes or until vegetables are tender, stirring frequently. Stir in crushed tomatoes, salt, if desired, and black pepper.

2. Stir in chicken. Reduce heat to low; cover and simmer 12 to 15 minutes or until chicken is cooked through.

MAKES 4 SERVINGS

NOTE: If jalapeño pepper is too mild-tasting, add ¼ teaspoon red pepper flakes.

QUICK & EASY CHICKEN QUESADILLAS

1¼ pounds skinless, boneless chicken breast halves, cut into cubes

1 can CAMPBELL'S® Condensed Cream of Chicken Soup **or** CAMPBELL'S® Condensed 98% Fat Free Cream of Chicken Soup

½ cup PACE® Picante Sauce-Medium

½ cup shredded Monterey Jack cheese

1 teaspoon chili powder

8 (8-inch) flour tortillas, warmed

1. Heat the oven to 425°F.

2. Cook the chicken in a 10-inch nonstick skillet over medium-high heat until well browned and cooked through, stirring often. Stir in the soup, picante sauce, cheese and chili powder and cook until the mixture is hot and bubbling.

3. Place the tortillas onto 2 baking sheets. Spread about ⅓ cup chicken mixture on half of each tortilla to within ½ inch of the edge. Brush the edges of the tortillas with water. Fold the tortillas over the filling and press the edges to seal.

4. Bake for 5 minutes or until the filling is hot. Cut the quesadillas into wedges.

MAKES 8 SERVINGS

SERVING SUGGESTIONS: Serve with PACE® Salsa and Mexican-style rice with beans. For dessert, serve chocolate frozen yogurt.

BAKED CRISPY CHICKEN

1 can (10¾ ounces)
CAMPBELL'S® Condensed
Cream of Chicken Soup
(Regular **or** 98% Fat Free)

½ cup milk

4 skinless, boneless chicken
breast halves (about
1¼ pounds)

2 tablespoons all-purpose
flour

1½ cups PEPPERIDGE FARM®
Herb Seasoned Stuffing,
finely crushed

2 tablespoons butter, melted

1. Stir **⅓ cup** of the soup and **¼ cup** of the milk in
a shallow dish. Lightly coat the chicken with
the flour. Dip the chicken into the soup mixture,
then coat with the stuffing.

2. Put the chicken on a baking sheet. Drizzle with
the butter. Bake at 400°F for 20 minutes or
until the chicken is cooked through.

3. Heat the remaining soup and milk in a 1-quart
saucepan over medium heat until hot, stirring
occasionally. Serve the sauce with the chicken.

MAKES 4 SERVINGS

INDEX

INDEX

ACKNOWLEDGMENTS

The publisher would like to thank the companies and organization listed below for the use of their recipes and photographs in this publication.

The Beef Checkoff

Bob Evans®

Campbell Soup Company

jarlsbergusa.com

McCormick®

Ortega®, A Division of B&G Foods North America, Inc.

Riviana Foods Inc.

Unilever

The Watkins Company

METRIC CONVERSION CHART

VOLUME MEASUREMENTS (dry)

1/8 teaspoon = 0.5 mL
1/4 teaspoon = 1 mL
1/2 teaspoon = 2 mL
3/4 teaspoon = 4 mL
1 teaspoon = 5 mL
1 tablespoon = 15 mL
2 tablespoons = 30 mL
1/4 cup = 60 mL
1/3 cup = 75 mL
1/2 cup = 125 mL
2/3 cup = 150 mL
3/4 cup = 175 mL
1 cup = 250 mL
2 cups = 1 pint = 500 mL
3 cups = 750 mL
4 cups = 1 quart = 1 L

VOLUME MEASUREMENTS (fluid)

1 fluid ounce (2 tablespoons) = 30 mL
4 fluid ounces (1/2 cup) = 125 mL
8 fluid ounces (1 cup) = 250 mL
12 fluid ounces (1 1/2 cups) = 375 mL
16 fluid ounces (2 cups) = 500 mL

WEIGHTS (mass)

1/2 ounce = 15 g
1 ounce = 30 g
3 ounces = 90 g
4 ounces = 120 g
8 ounces = 225 g
10 ounces = 285 g
12 ounces = 360 g
16 ounces = 1 pound = 450 g

DIMENSIONS

1/16 inch = 2 mm
1/8 inch = 3 mm
1/4 inch = 6 mm
1/2 inch = 1.5 cm
3/4 inch = 2 cm
1 inch = 2.5 cm

OVEN TEMPERATURES

250°F = 120°C
275°F = 140°C
300°F = 150°C
325°F = 160°C
350°F = 180°C
375°F = 190°C
400°F = 200°C
425°F = 220°C
450°F = 230°C

BAKING PAN SIZES

Utensil	Size in Inches/Quarts	Metric Volume	Size in Centimeters
Baking or Cake Pan (square or rectangular)	8×8×2	2 L	20×20×5
	9×9×2	2.5 L	23×23×5
	12×8×2	3 L	30×20×5
	13×9×2	3.5 L	33×23×5
Loaf Pan	8×4×3	1.5 L	20×10×7
	9×5×3	2 L	23×13×7
Round Layer Cake Pan	8×1½	1.2 L	20×4
	9×1½	1.5 L	23×4
Pie Plate	8×1¼	750 mL	20×3
	9×1¼	1 L	23×3
Baking Dish or Casserole	1 quart	1 L	—
	1½ quart	1.5 L	—
	2 quart	2 L	—